Written by Bodmin Dark
Edited by Philippa Wingate
Illustrated by Paul Middlewick
Designed by Zoe Quayle

With thanks to www.speeddater.co.uk

First published in Great Britain in 2004
Michael O'Mara Books Limited, 9 Lion Yard,
Tremadoc Road, London, SW4 7NQ
www.mombooks.com

A CIP catalogue record for this book is available
from the British Library

ISBN 1-84317-074-4

1 3 5 7 9 10 8 6 4 2

Made and printed in Great Britain
by William Clowes, Beccles, Suffolk

# THE LITTLE BOOK OF
# Speed Dating

# Contents

# Who? Why?
# What? Where?

# Is speed dating for me?

If you are a single person in need of a partner, speed dating is for you. So, what are you waiting for? Speed dating is a no-nonsense way of meeting a large number of potential dates in a short space of time. It's safe, fun and sociable, and doesn't come with the usual stigma of dating agencies or personal ads.

One of the biggest reasons for speed dating's rapid growth is its simplicity. It usually takes place in a bar or restaurant. An equal number of men and women get together and are given a few minutes to speak to each other, one-to-one. Then all they have to do is decide whether they would like to see each other again.

If you're nervous, sceptical or just plain scared, don't be. Stop making excuses, and read on.

# Who does it?

Speed daters are not desperate loners with no friends, too many cats and no social life (well, most of them aren't). They are normal people in their twenties, thirties and forties who aren't meeting new people through their work or immediate circle of friends. Many are people who just don't have the time to go out and meet potential partners.

Speed dating appeals to people from a huge variety of backgrounds and with vastly different personalities.

There are events organized for straight, gay and bi-sexual daters, sports daters, media daters, religious daters and students – so rest assured you should find a category to suit your tastes!

Many companies offer a variation on the basic speed dating theme. They might call it a different name, including fast dating, hurry dating, three-minute dating, six-minute dating, or even 30 dates in one evening. There's even speed dating in the dark, but essentially the procedure is the same.

# Why do people do it?

Repeat this mantra – speed dating is fun; speed dating is fun.

Quite apart from the possibility of finding a date, the evening can boost your confidence and give you a real buzz. Speed dating is fast becoming a socially acceptable way for single people to get together for a fun night out while meeting new people.

You can go along to an event on your own or with friends (about 60 per cent of men and 30 per cent of women go alone). At speed dating you are guaranteed to meet a large number of people, and since everyone is there for the same reason, it has got to be a less scary experience than approaching a complete stranger in a bar. Look on the bright side, you won't have to use or endure cheesy chat-up lines.

Unlike blind dates, you can find out if there is any chemistry between you and your date before going through the nightmare (and expense) of a whole evening with someone you couldn't care less about. Speed dating is also remarkably successful. With the chance to meet 20 to 30 people in one night, most companies claim that over 50 per cent of participants will meet someone with whom there is mutual interest in another date – and let's face it, these are higher odds than an average night in a bar or club.

# What are the drawbacks?

The major drawback of speed dating is that there is no 'quality control'. Events are typically advertised as attracting professionals, but daters can be from all walks of life. Unless you go to an event that has been specifically arranged for a niche group, such as media types or members of a particular religious denomination, companies have no screening as part of the registration process. Just like internet dating, you are meeting total strangers, and that can account for a lot of different 'types'. You might be sitting opposite someone gorgeous, only for the time to run out and find yourself stranded with someone you can't bear to look at, let alone talk to. Believe it or not, that's part of the fun. Just think, you will be the most sought-after person in the office the morning after, with horror stories of making conversation with monosyllabic morons. And, on a more serious note, there are always breaks during a speed dating evening to catch up with people you really like the look of.

There is also no guarantee of success. You may have a great evening and come up with half a dozen matches, or you may come away empty-handed and hoarse.

# Where do people do it?

There are now a large number of companies specialising in speed dating. You can find them on the internet or in newspapers and magazines.

Simply go to their website or give them a call and find out where and when the next event is on. Do make sure before registering for a particular evening that you have selected the right age group and cultural background (it can make for awkward dating if you turn up and everyone's twenty years older than you).

The events are often held in a closed-off area of a bar, function room or sometimes they can fill a whole venue. You will need to pay a fee for registration and you will probably have to pay for your own food and drinks on the night.

# What actually happens?

# What happens on the night?

Once you have booked your event, you will be sent an e-mail confirming the time and place at which you should turn up. The e-mail will also outline what you should expect. Read these directions carefully, making a note of any special requirements.

Speed dating normally begins in the early evening. When you arrive, you will need to register with the representatives of the speed dating agency. They will issue you with a name badge, a number, a 'scorecard' and pen. You might feel like you are back at school, but stay cool and persevere.

The scorecard is to help you keep track of everyone you meet. You will be very thankful for it by the end of the evening when you have met your thirtieth speed date. Names and faces tend to blur into one after a while.

You will be invited to have a drink

at the bar and there will be breaks throughout the evening in which you can get a drink and go to the loo. Some agencies even provide appetizers prior to the start of the event.

Once everyone has arrived, a representative will explain exactly how the evening's speed dating will work. You will be told where to sit and what to expect.

Then the dating begins. Usually women stay seated while men move from table to table. The dating is fast and the venue can often become a very loud, hectic place, so have your wits about you and a good selection of questions at the ready (see pages 59 to 81 for some advice about asking and answering questions).

A bell, buzzer or whistle will sound at the end of the first date, at which point the man must move to the next table (even if he thinks he has already found the girl of his dreams).

Three to ten minutes doesn't sound like a lot of time, but these are mini-dates to see if you might be interested in a full date afterwards. If you are not interested in the person sitting opposite you, a couple of minutes can seem like an eternity.

You might be surprised at just how much you can pick up about someone in such a short space of time. It might be just the way they speak or smile, something that makes you laugh, a maturity, intelligence or composure, or just good old-fashioned chemistry.

After each date, it's a good idea to mark the name and number of the person you have been speaking to on your scorecard and make a few notes about them so you can remember who they were. Useful things to write include notes on distinguishing features, items of clothing or memorable things they have said.

Either after the date or at the end of the evening, mark on the scorecard who you would like to see again. Don't tell anyone during a date whether you want to see them again, and don't let people see what's written about them or others. In haste you may well have jotted down some fairly tactless notes about certain people. Keep your scorecard face down on the table during each date.

# How long does it last?

The number of people you see in one evening fluctuates. Typically, it will range between ten and 25. The duration of the dates may range between three and eight minutes. So, including breaks, the event may last up to three hours. People often stay for a drink after the event.

Be warned, speed dating can be exhausting – there's a lot to take in and you are on display. But it is exciting and hopefully well worth the effort.

# Hey, good-looking!

# First impressions

As with most things in life, in speed dating first impressions count for a lot. With only a few minutes alone with each date, it's worth making an effort to impress. This doesn't mean that you have to have the looks of a supermodel, the brains of a Nobel Prize winner and the wit of Oscar Wilde, you just have to make the most of what you've got.

Remember, if you look your best you will feel good, and if you feel good you will be more confident.

Confident people, in dating as in life, are attractive people.

Wear clothes you feel comfortable in, but something that is smart enough to reflect the fact that you are on a date.

Some bars have their own dress code, such as no jeans or trainers, so check with the organisers before you go. Shorts, flip-flops or sneakers are out. Suits are generally acceptable if, as is usually the case, people are coming straight from work.

# Look the part

## Breath

If your speed date can smell your breath across the table, the chances are you will not get a tick. There is nothing more off-putting than 'dog breath'. So clean your teeth before you get to the venue and having some mints in your bag is a very good idea.

## Smell

How you smell says a lot about you and, in the worst case scenario, a lot against you. If it has been a hot day or you have just come from a workout at the gym, there is the danger that you might smell like the inside of a weight-lifter's jockstrap. Take a shower – you know it makes sense.

Remember to pack deodorant or scent. Wear a good, clean fragrance and apply just enough for someone standing close to pick up the scent, but not enough to knock them over backwards.

# Tips for women

You probably have your own sense of style, but here are some general tips.

## Clothes

Tasteful and simple are the key words when choosing your outfit. Avoid tarty, provocative outfits where everything is on show, but by the same token don't look frumpy or dowdy. Best to avoid ripped jeans, and see-though is generally considered a little desperate. Choose one area of your body you are happy to draw attention to, but never

'display' more than one area at
a time.

## Accessories
Keep accessories to a minimum. Less
is more. Resist the temptation to look
ghetto-fabulous by draping yourself
in gold. You don't want to have to
shout to be heard over your bangles.

## Underwear
Wear sexy underwear – even though
nobody will know you are wearing
it, it will make you feel better about
yourself and do wonders for your
confidence.

### Hair

Again, simple is probably best.
Resist the temptation to change your
hairstyle radically before the event –
you will feel self-conscious. Take a
brush so that you can tidy yourself
up if necessary.

### Body hair

The majority of men are not
attracted by body hair, so wax to
the max.

### Make-up

Use natural colours that complement
your skin, not full warpaint.

## Hands

Make sure your nails are neat, filed and painted, at least with a coat of clear polish. It shows you take care of yourself.

# Tips for men

## Clothes

If you are coming straight from work, a suit is fine. If you wear a tie, make sure it's a good tie – leave the Mickey Mouse one your mum gave you at home, and that goes for the Christmas socks too. In fact, resist the temptation to let your clothes talk for you. A clean, well-pressed shirt does wonders.

## Shoes

You can tell a lot about a man from the shoes he wears. Avoid trainers, hiking boots or sandals (especially if you are wearing socks). Don't wear shoes that are scuffed, dirty or in need of polish.

## Jewellery
Old Chinese proverb say: Man who wear too much jewellery look like second-hand car salesman.

## Underwear
Wear clean, comfortable underwear. No one likes to see a man picking at his pants every time he stands up – and throughout the evening you will be up and down like a jack-in-a-box.

### Hair

You probably have your own ideas about what looks good on you. But statistics insist that ninety per cent of women like a man who is clean-shaven.

Check your nose and ears for extra facial hair, and if your eyebrows run together you might want to think about investing in a pair of tweezers. The 'Missing Link' is rarely a good look.

### Hands

Make sure you clean your hands.

Get the dirt out from under your nails and cut them short – long nails look so suspect. Have no doubt, if you are sitting at a table with a woman, she will check out your hands, because you know what they say – large hands, large...

# Dos and don'ts

# Don't blow it

You have very little time to make a good impression, so it's worth bearing in mind some basic dos and don'ts. You'll kick yourself if the one person you wanted to tick your box doesn't because of a beginner's mistake.

# Do it!

• Do relax. Be yourself, be positive, enjoy yourself. Nervous wrecks and anxious sweats are a big turn-off.

• Do follow the guidelines (pages 30 to 41) on appearance and hygiene. Even if you are convinced your natural charm and good looks will win hearts and minds, the truth is probably that you need all the help you can get.

• Do have something to eat before you go, even if it is just a snack.

This prevents embarrassing intestinal noises, settles butterflies and stops the first drink going straight to your head. Garlic, raw onions or strong smelling foods are obviously not an ideal menu choice.

• Do wear clothes that fit properly; spilling out of clothes that are too small looks tacky and desperate at best, and at worst you'll look like you can't afford to dress yourself.

• Do switch off your mobile phone.

• Do remember to smile.

• Do maintain eye contact and show interest in the person opposite you throughout a date.

• Do have a number of questions ready (see pages 59 to 81). Don't just ask 'So, what do you do for a living?' every time you change partners.

• Do fill out your scorecard as you go. You have been warned – speed dating can reduce your mind to mush very swiftly.

• Do use the breaks to talk to people. If there is someone on whom you don't think you made the best impression during a date, use this opportunity to put it right.

• Do remember your manners. If you don't like the person you are sitting with, they might have come with a gorgeous friend who will be obliged to hate you if you disrespect their mate.

• Do play it safe when you meet up afterwards (there is some sound advice about this on pages 122 to 127). In a nutshell, it makes sense to meet in a public place, to tell a friend

where you are going and not to give
out your home address or phone
number.

• Do be honest with yourself about
whether you like a person or not.
Trying to match with everyone is a
waste of your time and theirs.

# Don't do it!

• Don't start drinking heavily before the event. The evening will go downhill very fast and dribbling has never been considered that sexy.

• Don't overdo it. Less is always more, whether it is a tan, aftershave or jewellery.

• Don't ask sexually explicit questions, use lewd language or say anything that might be interpreted as sexually threatening.

• Don't tell lies. You risk life getting very complicated otherwise. You will forget which person you told you were a brain surgeon and who thinks you are an international aid worker.

• Don't reveal intimate secrets or draw attention to defects, real or imagined — it's just too much information.

• Don't swear excessively, it's not attractive.

• Don't belch, fart or blow your nose loudly — for obvious reasons.

• Don't talk a subject to death, and it is usually best to avoid politics, astrology, UFOs and crop circles altogether.

• Don't talk with your mouth full.

• Don't ask your date if they think your outfit makes your bum look big.

• Don't talk about previous dates.

• Don't talk about your troubled upbringing or your dysfunctional family.

• Don't moan – it's boring.

• Don't talk ultra fast – it makes you sound nervous. But talking too slowly can make you sound stupid.

• Don't wear hats and sunglasses indoors. It simply looks pathetic.

• Don't act inappropriately – no over-the-top presents or declarations of undying love.

• Don't ask for your date's contact information – it makes you look like a stalker.

• Don't talk about ex-partners and what you would like to do to them.

• Don't have unreal expectations. Speed dating is a fun night out, but it might not lead to marriage.

# The art of good conversation

# Making conversation

Here are some general pointers on how to impress not overbear, how to charm not alienate.

Go into every conversation feeling good about yourself, it will make others feel good about you. Be proud of who you are and play to your strengths. Concentrate on the conversation you are having, not about the one you have just had.

Don't dominate the conversation – it's not all about you! You might think you are fantastic and you might want to tell the other person all about yourself, but wait until you are prompted to. People who can fill three minutes about themselves without even taking a breath risk appearing boring, conceited or just plain scary. That said, remember that a conversation is all about balance – if you play your cards too close to your chest or stay completely silent, people will think you are unfriendly, arrogant or shifty.

Try to remember to use the other person's name once or twice during the conversation (it is usually written on a name badge). This is a subtle form of intimacy. People respond well to the sound of their own name. It shows that you are concentrating and that you value their company.

Show interest, listen carefully, and focus your attention on the person you are sitting opposite. Resist the temptation to eye up the hottie at the next table. Given this encouragement, your date will reveal more about himself or herself, which will fuel conversation. Good listeners are always regarded by others as great company, no matter how little they actually say.

Keep it clean! This is not the time or the place to ask about someone's sexual preferences. If you do bring up sex, you will be remembered, but for all the wrong reasons.

# Questions, questions

The most frequently asked questions on a speed date are – 'What do you do?' 'Where do you come from?' 'Have you been speed dating before?' 'What do you think of it so far?'. It isn't rocket science to work out that these questions get very dull when you've been asked them twenty times.

It's worth having some more imaginative teasers up your sleeve to use when you sense the conversation's flagging. If you want to make an impact and find out more than the average speed dater, you need to make your date stop and think.

Everyone at the event is interested in meeting people to date, but if you are not romantically interested in the person you're sitting opposite, you might as well pass the three minutes in a fun and friendly way. You'd be surprised how interesting people can be if you ask the right questions!

# Types of questions

There are three basic types of question: closed, open and probing.

### Closed questions

Closed questions (for example 'Do you like the venue?') generally start with the words 'are' or 'do'. They can be answered with a simple yes or no. Closed questions can be good if you have strict criteria, such as 'Do you smoke?'. They are not very good if you want to find out about someone and get a conversation flowing.

## Open questions

Open questions (for example 'What do you think of the venue?') generally start with the words 'what', 'where', 'which', 'who' and 'when'. They encourage a longer, more interesting reply, and are, therefore, much better as conversation openers.

## Probing questions

Probing questions usually start 'how', 'why', ' in what way' or 'tell me more about'. These questions ask your date for a further explanation, and are great for eliciting a longer response and moving a conversation along. So, with all that in mind, here are a few questions you might ask:

- If you won the lottery, how would you spend it?

- Tell me the three most important things I should know about you?

- What hobbies do you enjoy?

- What do you do for fun?

- What was your most unusual date, and why?

- Do you have any pets?

- Do you have any phobias?

- Do you come here often (no, only kidding!)

- If you had three wishes, what would they be?

- What's your greatest claim to fame?

- Tell me which three adjectives your friends would use to describe you?

- Where are you from?

- Of which of your achievements are you most proud?

- What makes you happy?

- What do you do for exercise?

- If you were on a desert island what three things would you take with you?

- Choose four things you would put in a time capsule?

- What kind of restaurants do you like?

- Would you rather eat Chinese take-away with chopsticks or eat fish and chips with your fingers?

- What is your favourite animal, and why?

- What one thing would
  you most like me to know
  about you?

- If you could interview anyone
  living or dead, who would
  it be?

- What's your favourite place
  in the world, and why?

- What are your favourite
  indoor activities?

- What are your favourite outdoor activities?

- Where do you see yourself in five years' time?

- Describe your strengths and weaknesses?

- Which is your favourite room in your house?

- What do you do on a typical Saturday?

- What was the most recent film you saw?

- What is the most crazy thing you have ever done?

- What book are you reading at the moment?

- What was the funniest thing
  that has ever happened
  to you?

- Are you a morning or an
  evening person?

- Who do you most admire,
  and why?

- Where has been your
  favourite holiday destination?

- Have you ever had a life-changing experience?

- What's your favourite word, and why?

- What do you feel is the most important quality in a person?

- What would be the title of your autobiography?

- Which magazines do you read?

- Which TV programmes you enjoyed as a child do you wish they would put back on screen?

- Would you rather take a trip in a submarine or a space ship?

- What person has most influenced you in your life?

- Which person, alive or dead, would be your perfect dinner date?

- What was the most embarrassing moment in your life?

- What is your most prized possession?

- Which quality in someone most annoys you?

- If you had to choose a meal that best represented your love life, what would be on the menu, and where would you eat it?

- What made you decide to go Speed Dating?

- What would your mother say if she could see you now?

- Did you tell the people you work with that you were coming tonight? What did they say?

- Would you rather a picnic at the seaside or a three-course meal at an expensive restaurant?

- What would you cook for me if I came round for dinner?

- If you could have any job in the world, what would you like to do?

- What is your ideal way to spend a Sunday afternoon?

- What was the single greatest day of your life?

- If you could be someone else for a day, who would you be?

- What was your favourite subject in school?

- Which TV programme do you never miss?

- What's your earliest memory from childhood?

- Who is the most interesting person you have ever met?

- Which is your favourite season?

- What do you wish your parents had told you?

- If you could live anywhere in the world, where would it be?

- What kind of music are you into?

- Is there one thing you couldn't live without?

- What makes you laugh out loud?

- What's your favourite movie of all time?

- What CD is in your stereo at the moment?

- What did you get away with in school that you've still never told anyone about?

- Which birthday do you best remember and why?

- What song have you been humming today?

- Would you describe yourself as a natural flirt?

# Over to you

Jot down your favourite questions
and how you would answer them.

_____

_____

_____

_____

_____

_____

_____

_____

_____

_____

_____

_____

_____

_____

_____

_____

_____

# Body
# conscious

# Body language

Experts think that it takes us between two and four minutes to decide if we fancy someone. So, regardless of how incisive your questions are and how witty your responses, what really counts is body language. Almost every facet of our personality is evident from our appearance, posture and the way we move.

When we meet someone, we give them an impression of ourselves. Statistically speaking, 55 per cent of this impression is communicated through our body language, 38 per cent through the tone, speed and inflection of our voice, and only seven per cent is communicated through what we are actually saying.

When flirting, all of our senses are heightened, which means we are even more open to body language. If you don't know how to read body language, you're missing out on what's really going on. Surprise, surprise, women tend to be much better at reading body language than men. But the good news is that, whoever you are, you can get better at reading body language and sending out the right signals yourself.

Don't judge someone's body language on one thing alone. Someone sitting with their arms crossed might mean they are protecting themselves emotionally, but it might just be that they are feeling cold. Look for a number of signals. If someone has their arms crossed and they're frowning, leaning backward and yawning, it's probably time to go.

## Smile

There are no two ways about it, people are more attractive when they smile. That doesn't mean that you have to sit there with a big, cheesy grin on your face all evening – you will risk people thinking you simple or insane. A normal, friendly smile that reaches your eyes will do wonders. If you catch someone smiling at you while you aren't actually talking to them, especially with their teeth exposed, it's a pretty clear indication they think you are hot.

## Use your eyes

When we first register that we are attracted to someone, our eyebrows rise and fall. If they fancy us back, they will raise their eyebrows in return. If one person is attracted to another, their pupil size increases and so does their blink rate. If you want to send the right signals, blink more yourself. If the person likes you, they'll unconsciously try to match your blink rate to keep in time with you. Don't go too far, you may look like you have something in your eye.

Winking is an excellent way of sharing a joke or a private moment. Done right, it can be a turn on. Done wrong, however, and you can look like you have a nervous twitch.

While you are talking to your date, make sure you maintain eye contact at least some of the time. It's a good idea to hold eye contact just a fraction too long at one stage during the date. This will create a brief, intimate moment.

# Follow their eyes

When we look at someone in a business situation, our eyes will zigzag from eye to eye. When we look at friends, our gaze tends to drop below eye level and move in a triangle shape from eye to eye down to the nose and mouth. When we flirt, this triangle widens to include the body. The more intense the flirting, the more intensely we'll look from one eye to the other. If someone is watching your mouth while you're talking, it may indicate they want to kiss you.

# Be their mirror

Nothing will bond you with your date more effectively than mirroring their behaviour. If they lean forward to tell you something, lean in to meet them. If they sit back and sip their drink, take a sip of your drink too. We like people who are like us, so if someone is doing what we're doing, we feel they are on the same wavelength as us. However, don't imitate precisely or you risk looking as if you are making fun of them.

## Get to the point

Often, when someone is interested in you, they will point their body, feet or knees in your direction. However, if someone looks at you over a shoulder that's pointed in your direction then that is another sure sign.

## Stay calm

Don't fidget, chew gum, crunch ice or gnaw your fingernails. Fidgeting indicates anxiety or frustration, neither of which are very attractive qualities.

## Sit forward

In a noisy bar, you will probably find yourself leaning forward to listen to what the person opposite you is saying. This is a positive thing because sitting forward is a way of showing someone that you are interested in what they have to say.

However, always remain in your seat. If you stretch too far across to their side of the table, at best you will knock over a drink, at worst you will intimidate them.

## Don't touch

It is not appropriate during a speed date to play footsie or stroke the arm of the person you are talking to. It may be interpreted as overconfident or just plain slutty.

# Tips for women

As a woman, the key is to make yourself seem approachable. Nod and tilt your head, a clear signal that you're listening to what someone has to say. The more open you are, the more attractive you become. So expose your wrists, palms and the insides of your arms in their direction. Try not to sit with your arms crossed.

If you are enjoying a man's company, you can give him subtle hints that this is the case. Push out

your chest; toss back your head and
hair and smile; preen your hair or
clothing; flare your nostrils; blush, or
play with your shoe on the end of
your foot. Bear in mind that doing
all of these things together may make
you appear deranged.

# Tips for men

Confidence is one of the key factors used by women to rate a man during a first meeting. If you don't act confidently, you may appear awkward and your date will not feel comfortable in your company.

The good news is that speed dating is great for confidence-building. By the end of the night, even the shyest person will usually be chatting away quite happily about all sorts of things.

When standing during the breaks, try to stand with your feet six to ten inches apart, toes pointing outward. This will make you look relaxed and in control.

# Take a break

# Making the most of the breaks

Speed dating isn't just about the time you spend at the tables. Throughout the evening there will be breaks for you to get a drink or go to the loo. These can be perfect opportunities to go back and chat to someone you particularly like.

During breaks, speed daters tend to gather at the bar. Be friendly, smile and chat to others. If you are on your own, try to strike up a conversation with someone nearby. Don't worry at this stage about who you speak with. The important thing is that you appear confident, comfortable and, above all, friendly. If you can carry this feeling into the dates, you will appear much more attractive.

During breaks, a good way to show your confidence is to stand in the middle of the room or stay at the corner of the bar where you will meet more people and get served quicker (bartenders tend to gravitate toward the corners). The worst place to stand is near the wall or behind a table. While you are milling around, it's OK to look at other people. It's even good to get caught looking if you fancy someone. Most people look away when someone looks at them, but if you want to let that person know you are interested, smile, hold eye contact a moment longer, before you look away.

When you are standing with a drink in your hand, you can check out the other people present. However, the goal is to compliment someone by showing that you have noticed them;

don't size up their body as if it is a piece of meat. Make eye contact, then, quickly, in less than a second, pass your eyes down and then up over their body, then back to looking into their eyes. Be quick and unashamed of taking a glance. Just don't do it too often.

# Know when to stop

The idea of speed dating is to give someone a taste of who you are and leave them wanting more. Ideally you should stop flirting on a high point, while it's still fun, then your new friend will feel good when she or he thinks of you, and will want to see you again.

# What
# happens next?

# Ticking boxes

Once you have met everyone at the event, you will be asked to mark your scorecard with a tick to indicate who you would like to see again. Alternatively, you will be told to enter the details onto the company's website.

You only get one chance to enter your ticks. So before you do, it's worth pausing for thought. Every one of your fellow speed daters is on their best behaviour, and they are all trying to make the best impression they can. Try to be honest with yourself – speed dating is not the most natural way to meet people. The whole point of speed dating is that you can find out about people without the waste of time and money you might suffer on an unsuccessful date. That means that it's important to be selective when choosing who you would like to see again. Hopefully, you will have made a few notes on your scorecard and a few people will have made a favourable impression, but it's worth bearing a few things in mind before you put a tick next to their name.

- What did you really like about this person that made them stand out?

- Are you choosing this person just because they are good looking or rich?

- Did you share any common interests with this person?

- Are you just ticking this person to get something out of the evening?

- Could you have a serious relationship with this person?

At the end of the evening you may find yourself in conversation with someone and wish to tell them that you will tick their name on your scorecard. However, don't pressure them to tick your name too.

# Making a match

With everyone's results gathered in,
the organisers will compare the
scorecards and work out who liked
who. They do this by working out
which people have ticked each
other. This is called a 'match'. If
you tick eight people and four of
those people tick you, you will
receive four matches. You will be
sent confirmation of your matches
which will include contact details.
Then it is up to you to arrange to
see them again – or not.

Some speed dating companies will tell you the number of ticks that you received in total, and even the other speed daters who ticked you. They usually only provide this information once you have submitted your list of who you would like to see again.

When you have received your matches, have another think about exactly which ones you are interested in. However, don't wait more than three days after you receive your matches to make the initial contact.

E-mail is an excellent and safe

method of contacting someone, especially if you feel too shy to phone. Don't be tempted to give anyone your home phone number or mobile phone number until you have met them for coffee first.

Don't take it personally if your match does not respond to your e-mail. After the excitement of a speed dating evening has calmed, people sometimes get cold feet.

# Pre-screening

Don't go overboard straightaway. Instead of setting up a date right away, exchange e-mails for a day or two to get to know your match a little better.

E-mail is a great way to pre-screen your match before you waste your time on a date that will go nowhere. Have a couple of questions you really want to ask. Keep e-mails brief, but long enough to find the information you are looking for.

When you are ready, thank your match for e-mailing you, and say 'I am in the process of contacting all my matches right now' or 'I will know my schedule more next week if you would like to have a coffee or meet for lunch'.

# Coffee date

Once you have pre-screened all your matches, it's time to narrow your choices further. Ask yourself which of your matches you would really want to meet again. If you had five to ten matches and decided after pre-screening that you only have a real interest in three, contact those matches and set up a one-hour date – lunch or a coffee is ideal.

Keep the tone of your e-mail very casual, quick and light. If the match suggests dinner, tell them you are busy and you only have a small amount of time right now.

After you have had a chance to meet all your matches for a one-hour date, you will be able to tell if any one of them is really worth spending an evening of your time and money.

Send a friendly e-mail to your other matches, telling them that you enjoyed meeting them, but that you have decided that you aren't going to pursue the match further. Spare them the details, you don't have to tell them exactly why!

Don't take more than two weeks to get around to meeting for lunch or coffee. If two weeks have passed, you have to ask yourself, am I really interested in this person or am I just looking for a date for the sake of a date?

Decide from your lunch or coffee if you really want to see this person again. If so, call within a week to arrange a proper date, maybe a meal, or a trip to the cinema or the theatre.

# Stay safe

# Safe, not sorry

Remember – it's always best to be cautious, sensible and, above all, safe. Speed dating companies do not screen participants and regardless of where or how you meet someone, dating is always a gamble. Be careful who you trust and take your time getting to know someone before you put yourself in a vulnerable position with them.

It's a good idea to trust your gut instincts – when something feels wrong, it often is and when someone appears untrustworthy, they often are.

Always let a friend know where you are going on a date. Give your friend the contact details of the person you are meeting and carry a mobile phone when you are out on the date. Tell them what time you expect to be home and arrange for them to ring you to check you arrived back safely. Use text messages to keep your friend posted if you suddenly change venue or decide to stay later than expected.

Always meet your match in a public place. It's a good idea to choose somewhere you are known. Remember to keep the first meeting short – about an hour. Even though you've already met your date at the speed dating event, remember that you are still strangers. Meeting someone through speed dating is not the same as meeting them at a regular group activity or through a friend. Always stay in control on the date – don't drink too much and don't be tempted to throw caution to the wind.

Don't invite strangers into your home and don't go to theirs until you know them well. If you are driving to the venue of your date, make sure you each take your own car. Never get in a stranger's car. Make sure you have met someone a few times before allowing them to pick you up at your home address.

Avoid long walks or hikes in the country, bike rides or drives in remote areas. It is just common sense, really. Make sure you end the date while there are still other people present. In the longer term, you can usually spot a fake or a fraud, because they are generally inconsistent and will have strange patterns of communication. They will rarely provide direct answers to direct questions and will never introduce you to their friends, colleagues or family.

You can only expect others to be honest if you are honest with yourself. Don't tell lies and don't imagine you have fallen in love with the first person who agrees to see you. Take responsibility for yourself and respect the other person's wishes, even if you don't agree.

# Men, take note

Women have to be particularly careful about meeting a stranger. When you are with a date, be understanding of this and don't be pushy. Do not talk about sex and do not touch her other than shaking her hand.

Treat the woman you are meeting as you would like another man to treat your sister on a date. You wouldn't want her to feel uncomfortable. So don't drink too much, don't be loud, obnoxious or use foul language.

Michael O'Mara titles are available by
post from: Bookpost, PO Box 29, Douglas,
Isle of Man IM99 1BQ
Credit Cards accepted.
Please telephone 01624-677237
Fax: 01624-670923
E-mail: bookshop@enterprise.net
Internet: www.bookpost.co.uk
Free postage and packing in the UK.
Overseas customers allow £1 per paperback.

New, expanded 128-page editions,
95x85mm. All at £2.50 each
including postage (UK only).
The Little Book of Cockney
Rhyming Slang
- £2.50 - ISBN - 1-84317-027-2
The Little Book of Farting
- £2.50 - ISBN - 1-85479-445-0
The Little Toilet Book
- £2.50 - ISBN - 1-85479-456-6
The Little Book of Stupid Men
- £2.50 - ISBN - 1-85479-454-X

Original 96-page editions., 95x85mm
All at £1.99 each
including postage (UK only).
WAN2TLK? ltle bk of txt msgs
- £1.99 - ISBN - 1-85479-678-X
The Little Book of Crap Advice
- £1.99 - ISBN - 1-85479-883-9

The Little Book of Crap Excus
- £1.99 - ISBN - 1-85479-882-0
The Little Book of Pants
- £1.99 - ISBN - 1-85479-477-9
The Little Book of Pants 2
- £1.99 - ISBN - 1-85479-557-0
The Little Book of Bums
- £1.99 - ISBN - 1-85479-561-9
Get Your Coat - You've Pulled
- £1.99 - ISBN - 1-85479-891-X
The Little Book Of Sex Fanta
- £1.99 - ISBN - 1-85479-725-5

Cheque books
Sex Cheques
- £2.99 - ISBN - 1-85479-598-8,
70x200mm, 72pp
Sex Maniac's Cheques
- £2.99 - ISBN - 1-85479-434-5,
70x200mm, 72pp